THE WILD WEST

NOTORIOUS OUTLAWS

by Anita Yasuda

Content Consultant
John Barton
Principal Lecturer of History
Utah State University

Core Library

An Imprint of Abdo Publishing
abdopublishing.com

www.abdopublishing.com

Published by Abdo Publishing, a division of ABDO, PO Box 398166, Minneapolis, Minnesota 55439. Copyright © 2017 by Abdo Consulting Group, Inc. International copyrights reserved in all countries. No part of this book may be reproduced in any form without written permission from the publisher. Core Library™ is a trademark and logo of Abdo Publishing.

Printed in the United States of America, North Mankato, Minnesota
032016
092016

Cover Photo: AS400 DB/Corbis
Interior Photos: AS400 DB/Corbis, 1; Kenneth John Petts/Private Collection/Look and Learn/ Bridgeman Images, 4; Charles Marion Russell (1865-1926)/Private Collection/Peter Newark Western Americana/Bridgeman Images, 6; North Wind Picture Archives, 9, 28; American School, (19th century)/Private Collection/Peter Newark American Pictures/Bridgeman Images, 12, 23, 24, 45; Library of Congress/Wikimedia Commons, 15; Red Line Editorial, 18, 25; Leemage/ Corbis, 20; S400 DB/Corbis, 31; Corbis, 33; Everett Collection/Newscom, 36; World History Archive/Newscom, 39

Editor: Claire Mathiowetz
Series Designer: Ryan Gale

Cataloging-in-Publication Data
Names: Yasuda, Anita, author.
Title: Notorious outlaws / by Anita Yasuda.
Description: Minneapolis, MN : Abdo Publishing, [2017] | Series: The wild West
    | Includes bibliographical references and index.
Identifiers: LCCN 2015960527 | ISBN 9781680782578 (lib. bdg.) |
    ISBN 9781680776683 (ebook)
Subjects: LCSH: Outlaws--West (U.S.)--Juvenile literature. | Frontier and pioneer
    life ((U.S.)--Juvenile literature.
Classification: DDC 978--dc23
LC record available at http://lccn.loc.gov/2015960527

CONTENTS

CHAPTER ONE
Escaping the Law in the West . . 4

CHAPTER TWO
Robbers and Gentlemen
Bandits 12

CHAPTER THREE
Old West Gangs and Leaders . . 20

CHAPTER FOUR
Cattle Thieves and
Land Wars 28

CHAPTER FIVE
Women Outlaws of the West . . 36

Key Locations 42

Stop and Think .44

Glossary 46

Learn More 47

Index 48

About the Author 48

ESCAPING THE LAW IN THE WEST

It was 1877. Money had been taken from a Wells Fargo stagecoach in broad daylight. It was the work of a unknown bandit. The masked man had been armed. On a lonely stretch of road, the bandit had demanded that the driver give up the money. The holdup was not unusual. Life in the Wild West could be difficult and dangerous.

A masked bandit stealing money from a family in the West

Families from all over the country relocated to the West in the 1840s.

United States Expansion

Americans had been settling the land between the Mississippi River and California since the mid-1800s. But this land had not always belonged to the United States. In 1803, the country expanded. The third US president, Thomas Jefferson, approved the purchase of 838,000 square miles (2,144,520 sq km) of land from France. This deal pushed the western boundary of US territory from the Mississippi River to the Rocky Mountains. It was called the Louisiana Purchase.

Beginning in the 1840s, the United States grew even larger. In 1846, the United States and the United Kingdom divided the Oregon Territory. This land was west of the Rocky Mountains to the Pacific. After the Mexican-American War (1846–1848), the United States gained 525,000 square

Homestead Act

The federal government encouraged Americans to settle in the West. Starting in 1862, it offered people land through the Homestead Act. The act gave people 160 acres (65 ha) of land for free. In return, they had to live on the land for five years and build homes. Thousands of people jumped at the chance to own land. But as land was claimed, the government forced American Indians onto reservations. The reservation land was not good for hunting or growing food. Most Native Americans lost their land and the government refused to recognize their tribes as independent.

miles (1,360,000 sq km) of Mexican territory. That land is now Texas and most of the states in the Southwest.

However, the regions were already home to Native American tribes. Still, the promise of a better life drew Americans westward. It did not matter to them that other people already lived there. Americans believed it was their right to expand the nation. This idea was called Manifest Destiny. For native people, however, Manifest Destiny meant the loss of their traditional lands and their culture.

Flocking to the West

Many types of people went west. There were farmers, craftsmen, and teachers. Most people obeyed the law, but many did not. There were feuds between small ranchers and big land owners. Mining camps could be very violent. People could be killed over something as minor as a stolen shovel. Some men who had fought on different sides of the US Civil War (1861–1865) continued to fight with each other. Cowhands used their fists and knives to settle fights.

A sheriff leading a team of men through the frontier

The West also attracted cattle thieves, robbers, and gamblers. These people saw opportunity in the new towns springing up between the plains and the Pacific coast. There were miners and settlers to rob. There were horses to steal.

Law in the West

At the beginning of the Wild West period, many present-day states were part of larger territories.

The federal government sent officials to run them. It sent people called marshals to enforce federal laws. Marshals and their deputies had a lot to do to keep law and order. The large size of the western territories made them hard to police.

In many cases, one marshal was in charge of an entire territory. Marshals often traveled thousands of miles on horseback to do their job. Some towns were hundreds of miles from a court.

As towns grew, they hired sheriffs to take care of local crime. Often,

PERSPECTIVES
Louise Clappe

Louise Clappe lived in a mining town in California. From 1851 to 1852, she wrote to her sister about her experiences. Her letters explained the cruelty and danger of vigilante justice in the West. She described how a mob hanged a man they thought was a thief. The mob had surrounded him. They told the man what the charges were. But he did not understand. The man spoke only Swedish. He had been given no real trial. Yet in minutes, they decided he should die.

people did not wait for justice. They quickly took the law into their own hands. They hanged suspected criminals from trees.

But armed citizens could not stop every crook. Outlaws formed gangs and squared off with lawmen and private citizens in deadly gun battles. They quickly became known for their fast escapes. They were usually violent people. They used guns to rob banks and trains. Many innocent people died.

Newspapers and books published tales of their crimes. Authors often added to the stories to make them more exciting. The public loved the tales so much that some outlaws became legends.

EXPLORE ONLINE

This chapter identifies groups of people who did not obey the law and those who carried out justice. To learn more about how justice was handed out in the Wild West, visit the website below. What new details did you learn?

Frontier Justice
www.mycorelibrary.com/notorious-outlaws

CHAPTER TWO

ROBBERS AND GENTLEMEN BANDITS

Thieves made a living by stealing from settlers. They scooped up treasure from stagecoaches. Travelers' pockets were picked clean. Thieves found it useful to be skilled with a weapon. When trouble started, these outlaws wanted to be the only ones left standing.

There were, however, outlaws who never killed anyone. Some were said to have robbed from the

Joaquin Murrieta was known as Mexico's Robin Hood to those who supported him.

Dime Novels

Starting in the 1860s, exciting stories about the West were printed in paperbacks. The novels cost only a few cents. Much later, after the price increased, they became known as dime novels. They were written for young people and the working class. These tales about the American West turned outlaws into heroes. Some stories were about real people. Many depicted actual train robberies and bank holdups. But writers also added made-up details to make the stories more exciting.

rich to give to the poor. Others claimed they had been treated badly in the past, which led them to give up on trying to make an honest living.

Gold Country

In 1848, miners found gold in California. More than 300,000 people rushed in. They wanted to get rich.

In the 1850s, crime in the gold country was spreading. But lawmen frequently sought one man: Joaquin Murrieta. Stories spread of Murrieta robbing and killing white miners. He was angry after they drove him away from his mining claims. Today, people are not sure what parts of his story are true.

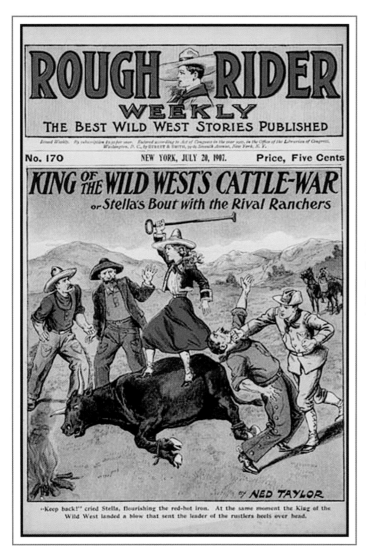

Most of the stories, adventures, and characters in dime novels were fictitious.

Some Spanish speakers saw Murrieta as a hero because he mostly robbed white settlers. After the Mexican-American War, people of Latin American descent began to lose their rights in California. Laws such as the Foreign Miners Tax of 1850 took away their freedoms. It kept anyone who wasn't white from mining.

Many other people wanted Murrieta stopped. California's governor offered a reward. In August 1853, lawmen arrived in Sacramento, California. They were carrying a head in a tin of alcohol. They said it was Murrieta's. But Murrieta's sister saw the head. She said it was not his. Whispers began that the real Murrieta had escaped to Mexico.

Several years later, stories of another Mexican hero spread in California. Tiburcio Vásquez became known for his charm as much as his crimes. Most of his victims were also white settlers. He didn't want them in California.

Stories spread of Vásquez giving stolen money to the poor. But newspapers called him a bloodthirsty villain. They said he robbed and killed people.

In the 1870s, Vásquez seemed unstoppable. The governor of California was fed up. On May 14, 1875, a posse of lawmen caught Vásquez. When he was in jail, fans came to visit him. He posed for photographs and gave interviews. But his charm didn't work on the judge or the jury. In 1875, Vásquez was found guilty of murder. He was hanged.

A Polite Thief

Stagecoach robbers worked the roads from Texas to California. One of the most successful bandits was Charles Earl Bowles, also known as Black Bart. He had once been a hardworking miner. But after 1875, he began robbing coaches.

Bart fascinated people. Even though Bart was a crook, he acted

PERSPECTIVES
Passengers' Perspective

Travel could be very dangerous in the late 1800s. Outlaws attacked not only coaches but also trains, which carried more money. By 1895, outlaws had robbed more than 100 trains. Hundreds of passengers and crew were put at risk. Outlaws threatened passengers. They shoved guns in their faces. They robbed and injured them. Some people died. In newspapers, holdups were called a "national disgrace."

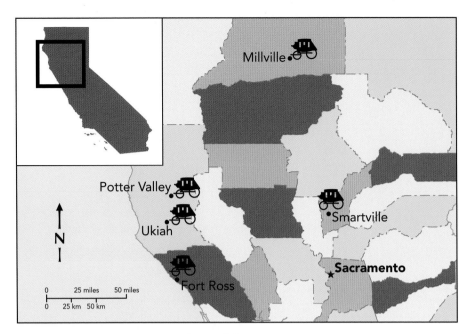

Black Bart Stagecoach Robberies

This map in California shows where Black Bart robbed several coaches. Many of these locations were less than ten miles (16 km) from towns. Why do you think he chose these locations? How might these locations have helped Black Bart rob coaches and make his getaway?

more like a gentleman. He asked politely for money. He left behind poetry.

At what would be his final holdup, Bart slipped up. He left behind a handkerchief. Detectives working the case located a witness who knew the owner of the handkerchief. The detectives found Bart and arrested him in 1883. They were surprised to meet their bandit. He was an elderly man in a nice wool suit.

On May 16, 1874, Tiburcio Vásquez explained in the *Los Angeles Star* how harassment by white settlers led to his life as a bandit.

> *My career grew out of the circumstances by which I was surrounded as I grew to manhood. I was in the habit of attending balls and parties given by the native Californians, into which the Americans . . . would force themselves and shove the native-born men aside, monopolizing the dances and the women. This was about 1852. A spirit of hatred and revenge took possession of me. I had numerous fights in defense of what I believed to be my rights and those of my countrymen. The officers were continually in pursuit of me. I believed that we were unjustly and wrongfully deprived of the social rights which belonged to us. . . . I was not permitted to remain in peace. The officers of the law sought me out in that remote region, and strove to drag me before the courts.*

Source: "Resistance in California." Digital History. Digital History, n.d. Web. Accessed October 6, 2015.

Back It Up

Tiburcio Vásquez uses evidence to support his point. Write a short paragraph describing the point he is making. Then write down two or three pieces of evidence Tiburcio Vásquez uses to make his point.

OLD WEST GANGS AND LEADERS

The period after the US Civil War was a time of great change. By 1869, the United States was linked by railroad from coast to coast. People saw the railroad as a way to travel faster.

Outlaws saw a different kind of opportunity. Trains carried passengers with valuables to steal. Trains also had safes with gold coins and cash. Outlaws risked everything to get at this fortune.

Wild west thieves taking money and possessions from passengers on a train

But robbing a train was not a one-person job. It took a gang, or a group of outlaws working together.

Detectives

In 1850, Allan Pinkerton started the Pinkerton National Detective Agency. It was the first private detective agency in the country. Railroad companies became some of his first clients. In the late 1800s, they needed security. Outlaws were robbing trains. Trains were much slower back then. Often, outlaws could just jump on at a lonely spot. There were also smaller crimes on trains, such as pickpocketing. The job of Pinkerton's detectives was to stop thieves from stealing.

The First Train Robbers

The first train robbers in the West were the Reno brothers. In October 1866, they burst onto a train in Indiana. With guns drawn, they grabbed more than $10,000 from a safe.

This was the beginning of the Reno brothers' crime wave. They terrorized trains throughout the Midwest. Once, they lit a fire on the tracks to stop a train. They threw a conductor off another. By 1868, the Renos were behind bars in Indiana. But local citizens wanted

Plenty of people were robbing trains in the late 1800s, but John and Simeon Reno were the first people to rob a moving train.

Jesse James and the Younger gang often committed their robberies in front of large crowds.

the men gone for good. A group broke into the jail and hanged them.

Feared and Celebrated

During the Civil War, Jesse James joined a group of men fighting against the Union. He was only 15 years old. His group was known as bushwhackers. They murdered and tortured Union soldiers. James also

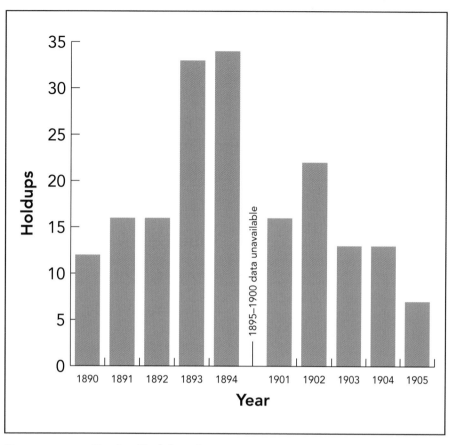

Passenger Train Robberies

This graph shows the number of train robberies per year between 1890 and 1894 and between 1901 and 1905. How would you describe train robbery activity before 1900? In 1902, the US Congress made robbing a train a federal crime. Based on this graph, what effect, if any, did the law have on railroad crime?

robbed banks and trains with his brother Frank and the Younger brothers.

Some people supported James. But he wasn't a hero. James robbed and murdered people for

The Other Side of the Law

In the 1800s, private detectives chased and caught outlaws. But they also had a bad reputation. Many people believed some detectives were worse than crooks. On January 26, 1875, a group of Pinkerton detectives surrounded the home of Jesse James's mother, Zerelda Cole James Samuels. The detectives threw a flare into the home. It exploded. It killed James's half-brother and blew off his mother's arm. People used that event to show how detectives were not always on the right side of law and order.

16 years. A member of his own gang killed him in 1882.

Butch Cassidy's Wild Bunch

Robert Leroy Parker was known as Butch Cassidy. In the late 1890s, Cassidy belonged to a gang of outlaws. They were so bold that the press called them "The Wild Bunch."

The Wild Bunch robbed banks and held up trains from Wyoming to Texas. In 1899, the governors of Colorado, Utah, Wyoming, and Idaho met to put a stop to them. That summer, the gang pulled off their biggest robbery. They stole $70,000 from a Rio Grande train near Folsom, New Mexico. Detectives from the Pinkerton National Detective Agency were soon on their trail.

After a few more jobs, Wild Bunch split up. Cassidy and fellow outlaw Harry Alonzo Longabaugh, also known as the Sundance Kid, took off for South America. In 1908, they were said to have died in a gunfight with troops in Bolivia.

FURTHER EVIDENCE

Chapter Three has quite a bit of information about outlaw gangs. What was one of the main points of this chapter? What evidence is included to support this point? Read the article at the website below. Does the information on the website support the main point of the chapter? Does it present new evidence?

Outlaw Hideouts

www.mycorelibrary.com/notorious-outlaws

CHAPTER FOUR

CATTLE THIEVES AND LAND WARS

The cattle business helped the West grow. A lot of money was made selling cattle to markets in the eastern United States. Merchants in the East were willing to pay ten times more than those in Texas. But there were no rail lines from Texas to these markets. So ranchers hired cowboys to drive cattle hundreds of miles to reach towns along the railroad.

A cowboy rounding up cattle in the West

The House

In 1874, James Dolan and Lawrence Murphy opened a bank and a store in Lincoln County, New Mexico. People called it "the House." Local farmers had to sell to and buy from the House because no other supplier was close by. In 1876, Alexander McSween and John Tunstall opened a competing store. Dolan and Murphy didn't want competition. They had Tunstall and McSween killed.

Cowboys came from many different backgrounds. Ex-soldiers, Native Americans, Mexicans, and African Americans all found work on the range. Many cowboys were honest and hardworking, but some were rustlers. Rustlers were thieves. They stole cattle and horses and sold them to whomever would pay the most.

The Kid

William Henry McCarty Jr. was known by many names. He is best remembered as Billy the Kid. He was in and out of trouble from the age of 15. In 1878, he became involved in a nasty cattle war in Lincoln County, New Mexico. Two groups of powerful men wanted to

Billy the Kid claimed to have killed 21 men, one for each year of his life.

control the cattle business. A rival group killed Billy's boss, John Tunstall.

Billy wanted revenge. He joined a posse of cowboys known as the Regulators. They set out to kill the men responsible for Tunstall's murder. When the fighting was over, Billy and other Regulators began stealing cattle all over the territory. New Mexico governor Lew Wallace wanted Billy caught, dead or alive. On July 14, 1881, Pat Garrett, sheriff of Lincoln County, ambushed Billy. He shot Billy dead. The outlaw was only 21 years old.

A Cattle Rustling Gang

Newman "Old Man" Clanton and his sons lived near Tombstone, Arizona. They were cattle thieves. Their neighbors, Tom and Frank McLaury, came along on these raids. They sold the beef to hungry miners and other customers.

But in 1881, a former Kansas City marshal came to town. His name was Virgil Earp. He became deputy

Doc Holliday was a dentist and a gambler before he joined the Earps in fighting the Clanton gang.

sheriff of Tombstone when lawlessness was at an all-time high.

Virgil's brothers Wyatt and Morgan took up different roles in the town. Sometimes their friend, Doc Holliday, helped them. Rustlers such as the Clantons soon became the Earps' enemies.

On the night of October 25, 1881, the two groups met at one of the saloons in Tombstone. They got into a heated argument. The next morning, the Clanton gang made plans to leave town. But the Earp brothers and Holliday stopped them at the O. K. Corral. Threats were made and guns fired. When the smoke cleared, the McLaury brothers and Billy Clanton were dead. Virgil and Morgan were wounded, but the lawmen left the scene alive.

This 1890 excerpt from the *Lincoln County Leader* was written by a person who knew Billy the Kid. In the letter to the paper, he wrote:

> *In regard to the guilt or innocence of Billy the Kid I will here state, that Billy himself . . . never denied that he was in the habit of stealing cattle from John Chisum, of Roswell, against whom he professed to have it claim, for wages I believe, which Chisum refused to pay, and hence he was determined to secure himself. He always said to me that he had never killed anybody, and never would do so except in self-defense. A couple of years before his tragic end he told me that during the time he was an outlaw in the Capitan Mountains all of Pat Garrett's deputies that tried to round him up were once in partnership with him stealing cattle from John Chisum.*

"The Lincoln County Leader. Volume, March 1, 1890, Image 1." Chronicling America. Library of Congress, 2015. Web. Accessed December 18, 2015.

Point of View

The writer views Billy the Kid in a favorable way. What does he say to create sympathy for Billy? Read the excerpt again. Do you agree? Why or why not?

WOMEN OUTLAWS OF THE WEST

omen held many important roles in the West. They worked on farms and cared for their families. They hired themselves out as maids and cooks. As Western towns grew, women became teachers and ran businesses.

There were also women who broke the law. They spied and stole for gangs. A few women led robberies. Nearly all women who became outlaws

Belle Starr in a portrait called "Queen of the Oklahoma Outlaws"

were married to one. Some had fathers or brothers who were criminals. Often, their adventures made them legends.

Belle Starr was one of the most famous female outlaws of the West. Born Myra Maybelle Shirley, she would go on to marry three different outlaws. It was written in papers that she robbed trains and banks with a gun in each hand. But the wild stories were mostly untrue.

She made money selling stolen horses with her second husband, Sam Starr. Outlaws used her farm in Indian Territory (present-day Oklahoma) as a hideout. In 1883, Belle and Sam were charged with horse theft. Belle had

Indian Territory

In 1828, the US government set up the Indian Territory. Present-day Oklahoma was part of this land. Beginning in 1830, Native American tribes from all over the country were forced to move there. The territory had its own courts and police. They couldn't interfere in cases that involved nonnative people. Outlaws took advantage of this to avoid the law. It became their favorite hiding place.

REWARD

$10,000

IN GOLD COIN

Will be paid by the U. S. Government
for the apprehension

DEAD OR ALIVE

of

SAM and BELLE STARR

Wanted for Robbery, Murder, Treason
and other acts against the peace

Wanted posters were used during the Wild West to catch outlaws.

to appear in court. Belle was lucky. She received a light sentence. She was out in less than a year.

In 1889, Belle was shot and killed on her way home from a trip. Her killer was never found. After Belle's death, a writer from the *National Police Gazette* was sent as a reporter to get the story.

His name was Alton B. Meyers. He made up many parts of her story. He called her the "Bandit Queen." His dime novel, *Belle Starr, The Bandit Queen, or the Female Jesse James*, turned Belle into a legend.

Arizona's Pearl

Pearl Hart was another legendary female outlaw. Born as Pearl Taylor in Canada in 1872, she married gambler Frederick Hart at age 19. The couple traveled to the 1893 Chicago World's Fair. There, Pearl discovered a Wild West show and loved it. Pearl left her husband and bolted for the West. While working as a cook in Arizona, she met miner Joe Boot.

In 1899, Hart learned her mother badly needed money. She came up with a plan to rob a stagecoach. She pointed a gun at the driver's head and another at the shocked passengers. Boot grabbed the money. Hart and Boot had never robbed a coach before. A sheriff and his posse caught up with them in no time.

Last of the Outlaws

The expansion of the United States throughout the 1800s drew many people—and outlaws— west. As the country continued to develop, crime didn't stop. But outlaws became viewed as myth and legend. The unlawful men, women, marshals, and gangs that once ruled the land soon became tales of the past.

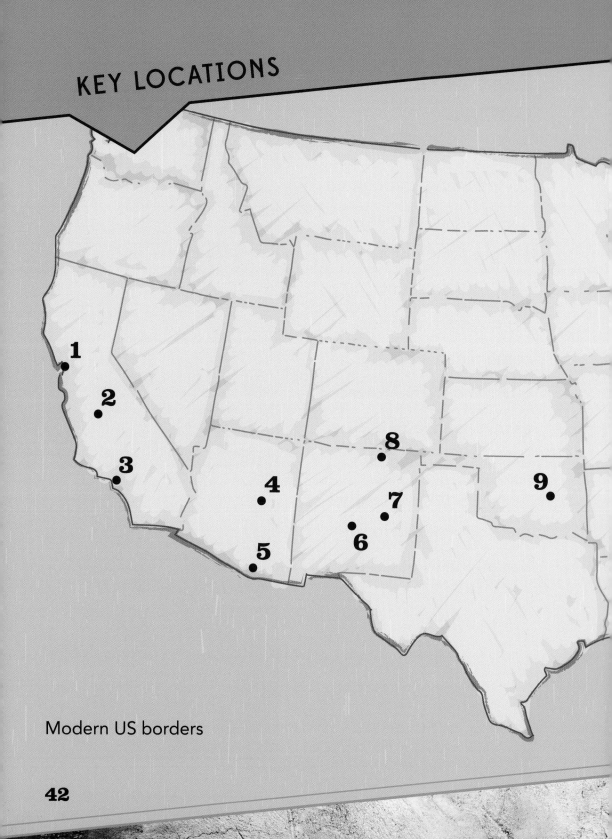

Modern US borders

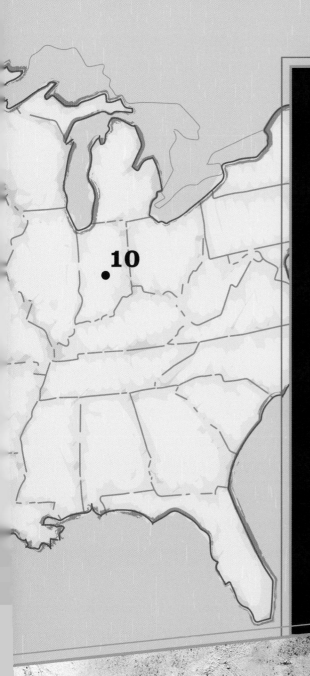

.**10**

Wild West Gunfights, Robberies, and Hideouts

1. **San Francisco, California:** Black Bart was apprehended in this city.

2. **Canuta Creek, California:** Lawmen claim this is where they killed Joaquin Murrieta.

3. **Los Angeles, California:** Tiburcio Vásquez hid in the hills north of the city.

4. **Globe, Arizona:** This is where Pearl Hart held up an Arizona stagecoach.

5. **Tombstone, Arizona:** The site of the Clantons' and the Earps' O. K. Corral shootout

6. **Lincoln County, New Mexico:** The site of the Lincoln County Wars

7. **Fort Sumner (Maxwell Ranch), New Mexico:** The site where Sheriff Pat Garett shot Billy the Kid

8. **Folsom, New Mexico:** The site of Butch Cassidy's largest train heist

9. **Eufaula, Oklahoma:** Belle Starr was murdered here on her way home.

10. **Jackson County, Indiana:** The site of the first US train robbery

STOP AND THINK

Tell the Tale

Imagine you are a stagecoach driver who must safely steer the coach through some of the most dangerous back roads in the country. Write 200 words about your passengers, your valuable cargo, and the dangers you encounter on your trip. How will you keep your coach safe? If you successfully complete the journey, will you continue to work for the coach line, or will you find a new job? Explain your reasons.

Dig Deeper

After reading this book, what questions do you still have about outlaws? Write down one or two questions that can help guide your research. With an adult's help, find a few reliable sources about outlaws that can help you answer your questions. Write a few sentences about what you learned.

Surprise Me

Chapter Five talks about women who became outlaws. Their actions often shocked people. What did you find most surprising about women outlaws? Choose two or three facts that surprised you, and write a few sentences about them.

Say What?

Learning about Western outlaws can mean seeing new words for the first time. Find five words in this book you'd never heard before. Use the glossary or a dictionary to help you find out what the words mean. Try writing the meanings in your own words. Use each word in a new sentence.

GLOSSARY

bushwhacker
a person who uses surprise tactics; also used to describe bands of outlaws during the Civil War

Civil War
a war fought from 1861 to 1865 between the Northern (Union) and the Southern (Confederate) states

Indian Territory
an area of land set aside for Indian tribes

marshal
a US marshal is a federal law officer, but a town marshal is only responsible for enforcing the law inside a particular town

posse
a group of people a sheriff assembles to keep the peace

reservation
an area of land set aside for Native American use

rustler
a person who steals cattle

saloon
a restaurant and bar

sheriff
the highest law enforcement official of a county

stagecoach
large carriage pulled by horses, used to carry mail or people

vigilante
a person who seeks justice by punishing a criminal outside the law

LEARN MORE

Books

Onsgard, Bethany. *Life During the California Gold Rush.* Mankato, MN: ABDO, 2015.

Onsgard, Bethany. *Life on the Frontier.* Mankato, MN: ABDO, 2015.

Yasuda, Anita. *Westward Expansion of the United States: 1901–1861.* Mankato, MN: ABDO, 2014.

Websites

To learn more about the Wild West, visit **booklinks.abdopublishing.com.** These links are routinely monitored and updated to provide the most current information available.

Visit **www.mycorelibrary.com** for free and additional tools for teachers and students.

INDEX

Arizona, 32, 40

Bart, Black, 17–18
Boot, Joe, 40

California, 6, 10, 14–18
Cassidy, Butch, 26–27
Civil War, 8, 21, 24
Clanton, Newman "Old Man," 32
Clappe, Louise, 10

Earp, Morgan, 33–34
Earp, Virgil, 32–34
Earp, Wyatt, 33–34

Hart, Pearl, 40
Holliday, Doc, 33–34
Homestead Act, 7

Indian Territory, 38
Indiana, 22

James, Frank, 25
James, Jesse, 24–26
Jefferson, Thomas, 6

Kid, Billy the, 30, 32, 35

Louisiana Purchase, 7

Manifest Destiny, 8
Mexican-American War, 7, 15
Murrieta, Joaquin, 14–16

Native Americans, 7, 8, 30, 38
New Mexico, 27, 30, 32

O. K. Corral, 34
Oklahoma, 38

Pinkerton National Detective Agency, 22, 26–27

Reno brothers, 22

stagecoach, 5, 13, 17, 40
Starr, Belle, 38–40

Texas, 8, 17, 26, 29
Tunstall, John, 30, 32
train, 11, 14, 17, 21–22, 25–27, 38

Vásquez, Tiburcio, 16–17, 19

Wells Fargo, 5

Younger brothers, 25

ABOUT THE AUTHOR

Anita Yasuda is the author of many books for children. She enjoys writing biographies, books about science and social studies, and chapter books. Anita lives with her family in Huntington Beach, California.